— THE —
MOJAVE DESERT

ABANDONED CALIFORNIA

—THE—
MOJAVE DESERT

ANDY WILLINGER

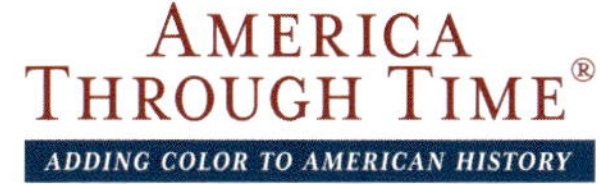

For Ericka

America Through Time is an imprint of Fonthill Media LLC
www.through-time.com
office@through-time.com

Published by Arcadia Publishing by arrangement with Fonthill Media LLC
For all general information, please contact Arcadia Publishing:
Telephone: 843-853-2070
Fax: 843-853-0044
E-mail: sales@arcadiapublishing.com
For customer service and orders:
Toll-Free 1-888-313-2665

www.arcadiapublishing.com

First published 2020

Copyright © Andy Willinger 2020

ISBN 978-1-63499-237-4

Typeset in Trade Gothic
Printed and bound in England

CONTENTS

ACKNOWLEDGMENTS

Special thanks to: Dr. Ericka Hofmeyer, Doris Robbins, Kurt Willinger, Doris Willinger, Jeremy Willinger, Matthew Willinger, Katie Willinger, Dana Stein Willinger, Michael Tingoli, Lucy Hofmeyer Lancaster, Helena Hofmeyer Lancaster, Fiona Hofmeyer Lancaster, Scott Schaffer, Mark Warren, Todd Christensen, John Edward Robinson III, Jordan Perzik, Kevin Lynch, Richard Misrach, Walter Feller and mojave-desert. net, Kim Stringfellow, Mojave Desert Land Trust, Explorers of the Mojave Desert, and the Yucca Valley Alano Club.

INTRODUCTION

In 2011, archaeologists, using high-resolution satellite imagery, discovered the ruins of the lost city of Tanis—the former northern capital of Egypt, which had vanished beneath the sands of the Sahara. The remains of a vast city grid with roads, houses and temples were found hiding under just a few inches of desert soil, completely invisible to the eye. When water became scarce, the people of Tanis moved on. Their homes, hopes and dreams were left behind to be reclaimed by nature and obscured by time.

In Southern California's Mojave Desert, a similar kind of entropy is occurring. Settlers have long ventured into the Mojave, seduced by its capacious horizons and fragile beauty, only to be abased by the intense heat, bone-dry terrain and maddening isolation. Industry, intent on extracting the land of its essence, set up operations, then walked away when there was nothing worth taking left. In many cases, natural erosion and decomposition have made it hard to tell that these projects, large or small, were ever there.

The Mojave Desert occupies nearly 48,000 square miles and its western boundaries are confined by the Tehachapi, San Gabriel and San Bernardino Mountains. The Mojave is also defined by the natural presence of the Joshua tree (*yucca brevifolia*), a tree-like yucca plant which only naturally propagates in this region. The Mojave is the hottest and driest desert on the continent, with less than two inches of rainfall annually on average. Temperatures generally range from highs of 95°-105°F in the summer, with lows of 20°-30°F in the winter. Much of the Mojave has an altitude of over 2,000 feet, and these areas are generally known as the High Desert. It also includes the lowest and hottest spot in North America, Death Valley, which has temperatures which routinely extend past 120°F. Joshua Tree National Park and the Mojave National Preserve are also located in the Mojave Desert. While it is hard to imagine the possibility of humans living in this region without air conditioning, the Mojave Desert has a rich history of people doing just that.

The Mojave can be paradoxically considered an urban desert, as its identity has been forged by the megalopolis of Los Angeles to the west, and Las Vegas to its east. As such, many of the settlers in the Mojave originated from the sprawl of the Los Angeles area, and the development of Las Vegas created jobs and opportunities along the way. In the 1920s, Los Angeles was connected to the rest of the United States by one of the original highways, U.S. Route 66, which cuts straight through the Mojave. As a major connector to those travelling west, towns surrounding Route 66 sprung up and prospered economically. By the late 1950s, however, businesses along Route 66 began to decline due to the creation of the national Interstate Highway System. The majority of these communities and businesses were circumvented by much larger, more efficient roadways. The allure of a radio hit song urging its listener to "(Get Your Kicks on) Route 66" proved incapable of maintaining their prosperity. Today, remnants of those "kicks" are hard to find, as most of the route's quirky diners, service stations, and motor lodgings have been completely demolished or abandoned. The harsh economics, compounded by the unforgiving climate of the Mojave, made it impossible for these depleted communities to survive.

The Mojave Desert has been gifted with abundant mineral deposits, and many of its early residents were settlers pursuing mining prospects and operations. By the 1860s, Gold Fever had spread south from the Sierra Nevada as large deposits were found throughout the desert region. Mines, mills and the communities to support them sprung up in the Mojave, searching not only for gold, but also silver, copper, tungsten, borax, zinc, and other minerals. By the end of the 1970s, most of the mines ceased operations and the residences of its workers were abandoned, as the cost of mining had become greater than the value of the elements extracted.

The abandoned buildings, vehicles and artifacts of the Mojave's once vibrant past are steadily deteriorating from the unforgiving climate. As a result, areas like the forsaken homesteads of Wonder Valley and the dehydrated Owens Valley have become fascinating contradictions. These sites seem simultaneously depleted yet majestically audacious in their quiet desolation. They have become meaningful, unintended statements in the tradition of land artists like Michael Heizer, Robert Smithson and Walter De Maria. These sites and monuments should be seen not only as vibrant, ephemeral artworks of minimal beauty, but as testament to the impact on nature by humanity. Undaunted, the Mojave Desert continues to brashly flaunt its skill in overcoming man's attempts to conquer it.

In the Mojave Desert, numinous, mystical experiences are not as rare as one might think. The numinous is a part of the whole artistic experience for the desert artist.
James Stanford

1

JOSHUA TREE AND YUCCA VALLEY

In this glare of brilliant emptiness, in this arid intensity of pure heat, in the heart of a weird solitude, great silence and grand dissolution, all things recede to distances out of reach, reflecting light but impossible to touch, annihilating all thought and all that men have made to a spasm of whirling dust far out on the golden desert.

Edward Abbey

California State Route 62 ascends northwards up a mountain past Desert Hot Springs from Interstate 10. After the first steep grade, the motorist gets the feeling they have traversed into a different land. The entrance to the town of Morongo Valley is a sparsely populated gateway to the High Desert of California. Continuing north up another very steep hill, the unique *yucca brevifolia* starts to become visible in the surrounding terrain. Continuing upward, these spindly Joshua trees seemingly take over the landscape in much greater size and frequency. The top of the hill indicates the driver's arrival into the town of Yucca Valley, which, at about 22,000 residents, serves as a hub for the entire Morongo Basin, with supermarkets, auto dealerships, and the area's only Walmart megastore.

The next town on Route 62 is Joshua Tree, which is the home of the famed Joshua Tree National Park—a vast, stunning landscape which attracts about three million visitors each year. Well-known for its mystical vibes and jaw-dropping beauty, the "Monument," as it is still referred to by locals, was the home of hundreds of mines, mills and settlements from the 1860s through the Second World War. While many of these sites have deteriorated into invisibility or have been remediated for public safety, the remnants of some of the old buildings and vehicles still stand off of the main park thoroughfares.

In the rural areas of Joshua Tree and Yucca Valley, some spectacular abandoned structures can still be discovered. While the area is facing rapid development, the harshness of the Mojave Desert climate and the obscurity of the area can be too unforgiving to overcome.

Mesa Shack, Joshua Tree. 2016

Sectional Sofa. Joshua Tree. 2016

Pool & Tennis Club. Yucca Valley. 2019

Ryan Ranch Tank. Joshua Tree NP. 2010

Wonderland Ranch House. Joshua Tree NP. 2012

Old Truck. Wonderland Ranch, Joshua Tree NP. 2012

Wheel, Old Truck. Wonderland Ranch, Joshua Tree NP. 2012

Ticket Booth. Sky Drive-In. Yucca Valley. 2016

Cash Register. Sky Drive-In. Yucca Valley. 2016

Beetle Barrier, Joshua Tree. 2016

Sonora House. Joshua Tree. 2016

Abandoned Camper. Joshua Tree. 2013

Futuro House. Joshua Tree. 2019

White Chair. Joshua Tree. 2016

2

WONDER VALLEY

I used to think that only people who were crazy were attracted to the desert, but once you've lived there, you become that way anyway.

James Turrell

As you travel east through the Morongo Basin along California State Route 62, signs of civilization drop off greatly after the town of Twentynine Palms. Shortly after passing the north entrance of Joshua Tree National Park, motorists are greeted by a startling road sign with bullet holes in it: "NEXT SERVICES 100 MILES." The concept of no gasoline stations, no restrooms, and most importantly, no water, is hard to fathom. This is the gateway to Wonder Valley, an unincorporated area of about 150 square miles of desolate beauty.

Most of Wonder Valley was undeveloped until the U.S. Congress approved the Small Tract Act of 1938, which leased and transferred ownership of small parcels of low-value land at almost no cost to citizens who were willing to build a simple dwelling on their claimed plot. By the early 1940s, the allure of seemingly limitless space and a deal too good to be true caused a sizeable land rush. By the end of World War II, thousands of humbly sized "jackrabbit homesteads," as they were known, sprung up on five-acre parcels, dotting the vast valley with a sense of hope and limitless potential.

That hope would not prevail for long. Lack of infrastructure, severe isolation, and difficulty in acquiring water proved too much for many of the original settlers. As Wonder Valley creeps down to one of the lowest elevations in what is considered the High Desert (1,500 feet), it gets noticeably hotter than the rest of the Morongo Basin. By the twenty-first century, over 2,500 of the homesteads were left abandoned or in severe disrepair, which caused San Bernardino County to fund and encourage their demolition. The challenges of frontier living proved too difficult for many, despite the low cost and spectacular terrain.

Today, Wonder Valley is home to a small, well-dispersed community of less than 700 misanthropes, artists, spiritual seekers, doomsday-preppers, UFOlogists and normal citizens. Many of the original mid-century cabins still stand in various states of decrepitude. It holds the largest collection of abandoned buildings still standing in the Mojave Desert by far. The glory and the heartbreak of the entropic process is on full display, as many of the homesteads and vehicles have been ravaged by vandalism, weather and time.

Exploration of these simple structures on this moon-like terrain can reveal clues to the unique experiences of the pioneers who settled the Mojave. Wonder Valley is a testament to the tenacity of the American entrepreneurial spirit, and how it's hopes and dreams can go awry.

Next Services. Wonder Valley. 2019

Green House. Wonder Valley. 2014

Slant House. Wonder Valley. 2014

Television Shack. Wonder Valley. 2016

Window, Meriwether House. Wonder Valley. 2015

Apex House. Wonder Valley. 2014

Disaster. Wonder Valley. 2014

Fleck Fusebox, Wonder Valley. 2014

Testament. Wonder Valley. 2014

Off the Hook. Wonder Valley. 2014

Eames House #3. Wonder Valley. 2015

Cabinet. Wonder Valley. 2016

Zenith. Wonder Valley. 2014

Gold Chair. Wonder Valley. 2014

Sanskrit Cabin. Wonder Valley. 2015

Blue Car. Wonder Valley. 2015

Blue Car Seats. Wonder Valley. 2016

Compadre House #2. Wonder Valley. 2015

Couch and Smoke Tree. Wonder Valley. 2015

Black House, Wonder Valley. 2016

Until The Very End. Wonder Valley. 2014

Yellow Mask. Wonder Valley. 2015

Interior, Licon Street Cabin. Wonder Valley. 2015

Wall Studs. Wonder Valley. 2015

Red House. Wonder Valley. 2018

Four Tires, Wonder Valley. 2015

Outhouse, Wonder Valley. 2016

Green Room, Cactus Jack Corner. Wonder Valley. 2015

Pink House #1. Wonder Valley. 2014

Jaguar Mark VII. Wonder Valley. 2018

The Right Angle. Wonder Valley. 2015

Crooked Cabin, 2-Mile Road. Wonder Valley. 2018

Crooked Window. 2- Mile Road. Wonder Valley. 2018

Basketball Court, Wonder Valley. 2012

3

THE CAR WASH

Desert is simply that: an ecstatic critique of culture, an ecstatic form of disappearance.

Jean Baudrillard, *America*, 1989

Hidden in the remote areas of the Mojave Desert's Joshua Tree National Park are some truly unexpected and spectacular artefacts of the Mojave's forgotten history. The eastern portion of the park is not as widely visited by tourists. It is considered an ecotone—a transitional area from the Mojave Desert to the Colorado Desert ecosystem. The dominance of Joshua trees and Mojave yuccas across the landscape diminish, yielding to a preponderance of creosote bushes and cholla cactus at lower elevations.

From Pinto Basin Road, heading north about 11 miles down a sandy, unpaved trail, then hiking more than a mile into the capacious Pinto Basin, a unique collection of about ten forsaken cars and trucks lie embedded in a dry wash about 100 yards from abandoned mining equipment. Although the Pinto Basin is mostly flat with sparse vegetation, these vehicles cannot easily be seen from a distance.

Dubbed the "Car Wash" by local explorers, the startling sight of these eroding *circa*-1950 vehicles half-buried into the desert floor is hard to comprehend. How could there be an upside-down Cadillac on this rugged plain? No logical or historical explanation is known as to why these vehicles would end up like this in such a desolate and obscure location. The Car Wash remains one of the great mysteries of the Mojave Desert.

Monolith. 2016

Car Wash Lineup. 2016

Sedan Sunset, 2016

1949 Cadillac Series 62 Sedan. 2016

Headlight. 1951 Ford F100. 2016

Interior, 1951 Ford F100. 2016

Embedded Wagon. 2016

4

ANTELOPE VALLEY AND NORTH MOJAVE

Water, water, water … There is no shortage of water in the desert but exactly the right amount, a perfect ratio of water to rock, water to sand, insuring that wide free open, generous spacing among plants and animals, homes and towns and cities, which makes the arid West so different from any other part of the nation. There is no lack of water here unless you try to establish a city where no city should be.

Edward Abbey, *Desert Solitaire: A Season in the Wilderness*

On the northern edge of Los Angeles County is the western boundary of the Mojave Desert. Travelling north on California State Route 14 over the expansive Tehachapi Mountains yields a spectacular view of the Antelope Valley and the city of Palmdale. The valley levels off at about 2,500 feet as Joshua trees become visible, with broad vistas and abundant sagebrush on the desert floor.

Populated by various cultures for over 10,000 years, the Antelope Valley was long a well-established trade route for Native Americans and settlers heading west to the coast of California. The neighbouring cities of Palmdale and Lancaster, which boasts a combined population of over 500,000 residents, have become a bedroom suburb for Greater Los Angeles, despite the very long commute.

Aside from Palmdale and Lancaster, Antelope Valley is sparsely populated and repeated attempts to develop the region agriculturally were hampered by issues providing adequate water supply. Numerous mineral extraction operations, ranches and planned communities were established and then forsaken either due to lack of water or economic viability.

Since the mid-twentieth century, the area has been dominated by the aerospace industry and the colossal Edwards Air Force Base, which includes the classified Lockheed Skunk Works and U.S. Air Force Plant 42. Hundreds of local contracting firms are involved with aircraft maintenance and manufacturing, and the remnants of inevitable obsolescence are evident throughout the valley. Due to the cheap land and dry conditions, the Mojave Air and Space Port has become a major boneyard to store surplus commercial aircraft. Dozens of jet airliners in various states of disrepair sit idle, awaiting their fate for either refurbishment or salvage. The Southern California Logistics center (formerly George Air Force Base) in Victorville also has large amounts of commercial jets in storage. As a result, random aircraft parts, large and small, are baking in the hot Mojave sun throughout the Antelope Valley in a multitude of aviation salvage and junkyards.

The areas north of Antelope Valley are some of the bleakest, eeriest and most beautiful parts of the Mojave Desert, and is the gateway to Death Valley National Park. While still part of the Mojave, the telltale Joshua trees virtually vanish, and several large valleys lie in between mountainous terrain. Areas such as Searles Valley, which has an abundance of minerals, has seen its mining heyday come and go. The Owens Valley, at the northernmost tip of the Mojave Desert, was once an agricultural hub with fertile farmland around the fresh waters of Owens Lake. In the early twentieth century, the Los Angeles Department of Water and Power created an elaborate aqueduct system that diverted water from the Owens Valley to Los Angeles, leaving farmers in uproar over inadequate supply to maintain their crops. These real-life water wars inspired the plotline for the 1974 film, *Chinatown*.

By the 1950s, Owens Lake had mostly been reduced to a drained, polluted alkali flat, with poisonous dust threatening the air of the entire region. As a result, most of the farms and residences in the Owens Valley have since been either abandoned or sold.

Fuselage. Adelanto, CA. 2014

Two Tails. Adelanto, CA. 2014

Red Corner, Victorville, CA. 2014

Chicken Farm. Helendale, CA. 2015

Nothing Even Mattress. Victorville, CA. 2014

Flight Deck, El Mirage, CA. 2017

Stone Cabin. Wilsona Gardens, CA. 2019

240th Street House. Palmdale, CA. 2019

Jet Trash. El Mirage, CA. 2019

Two Noses. El Mirage, CA. 2019

Standard Hill Cabin. Mojave, CA. 2019

Porch, Standard Hill Cabin. Mojave, CA. 2019

Boneyard, Mojave Airport. Mojave, CA. 2019

Alkali Bloom. Owens Valley, CA. 2018

Trashed Trailer, Olancha, CA. 2018

Doll Head. Trona, CA. 2014

Rustic Motel. Olancha, CA. 2018

Stone Cabin. Water Spout Gulch, CA. 2018

5

ROUTE 66

And 66 goes on over the terrible desert, where the distance shimmers and the black center mountains hang unbearably in the distance. At last there's Barstow, and more desert until at last the mountains rise up again, the good mountains, and 66 winds through them. Then suddenly a pass, and below the beautiful valley, below orchards and vineyards and little houses, and in the distance a city. And, oh, my God, it's over.

John Steinbeck, *The Grapes Of Wrath*

Since its creation in 1926, U.S. Route 66 has been one of the most well-known and romanticized paved roads in the United States. Originally connecting Chicago with Los Angeles, it became one of the main thoroughfares of the west and was widely described as the Main Street of America, or the Mother Road, as dubbed by author John Steinbeck. From the Arizona border westward, Route 66 slices the Mojave almost in half, and it spawned the creation of unique road-based businesses and culture to support the voluminous car and truck travel through the desert.

Route 66 started to decline in 1956 when President Dwight D. Eisenhower signed the Interstate Highway Act, which circumvented the simple roadway with modern, multi-lane highways that could accommodate higher volume and greater speeds. As a result, the distinctive motor lodges, service stations, restaurants and the communities that served them rapidly declined.

By the twenty-first century, many of the original structures along Route 66 through the Mojave had been completely demolished. Entire towns along the route, such as Bagdad, Siberia and Chambless, have virtually been erased from existence and the map. The few remaining structures stand as monuments from the golden age of American motoring and a much simpler time.

Whiting Brothers Gas Station. Newberry Springs, 2019

Henning Motel Sign Newberry Springs, CA. 2019. Formerly the motel location used in the 1987 movie *Bagdad Cafe*, it has now been demolished. Only the sign remains.

Not Responsible. Ludlow, CA. 2015

Sentinel. Ludlow, CA. 2015

Airfield Hangar. Amboy, CA. 2016

Roy's Motel & Café. Amboy CA. 2010

Roy's Motel & Café Sign. Amboy CA. 2010

Amboy School. Amboy, CA. 2015

Road Runner's Retreat. Chambless, CA. 2015

6

MINES AND MILLS

The desert was always there, a patient white animal, waiting for men to die, for civilizations to flicker and pass into the darkness. Then men seemed brave to me, and I was proud to be numbered among them. All the evil of the world seemed not evil at all, but inevitable and good and part of that endless struggle to keep the desert down.

John Fante, *Ask the Dust*, 1939

The Mojave Desert in California is a vast and sparsely settled region with a brutal climate, mountainous terrain and few sources of water. But that did not stop the early explorers from attempting to extract the abundant minerals which occur naturally throughout the terrain. Gold was first discovered in the Mojave in 1848 in a quartz vein at Salt Spring along the Mormon Trail in San Bernardino County. In the following years, thousands of prospectors and miners descended on the Mojave, setting up operations to extract and process not only other precious metals like silver, zinc and copper, but also other coveted minerals like potash, dolomite, limestone, borax and salt.

As the value and demand for these minerals decreased, and the cost of extraction climbed, many of these mining enterprises were abandoned, in many cases with the minerals still existing in abundance. While several of these mines were deserted with valuable equipment and vehicles still left in place, a great number of them have been remediated to the point that it is very difficult to tell that they ever existed. Although most of the dangerous mine shafts and pits have been sealed, exploring these sites can still be extremely perilous.

Peephole. Old Dale Mine. Old Dale, CA. 2014

Mine. Old Dale, CA. 2014

Silver Queen Mine. Mojave, CA. 2019

Platform. Old Dale Mine. 2014

Limestone Kiln. Chubbuck, CA. 2015

Detail, Limestone Kiln. Chubbuck, CA. 2015

Gold Rose Well. Pinto Basin, Joshua Tree NP. 2015

Stove, Gold Rose Mill. Pinto Basin, Joshua Tree NP. 2016

1939 Chevy Pickup. Gold Rose Mill. Joshua Tree NP. 2015

Rear View, 1939 Chevy Pickup. Gold Rose Mill. Joshua Tree NP. 2016

Ramp. Gold Rose Mill. Joshua Tree NP. 2016

Funnel. Gold Rose Mill. Joshua Tree NP. 2016

Mission Mill Tank #3. Pinto Basin, Joshua Tree, CA. 2014

Chloride Trench. Bristol Dry Lake. Near Amboy, CA. 2014

7

OTHER DESERT CITIES

A cactus doesn't live in the desert because it likes the desert; it lives there because the desert hasn't killed it yet.

Hope Jahren

There's a self-effacing joke in the smaller communities of the Mojave Desert to generically refer to their lesser-populated towns as "other desert cities." This sarcasm is derived from highway signs which say the road is heading toward a city, such as Indio, and also "Other Desert Cities," intimating that there's something else there, but not worth putting up a sign for.

This chapter is a collection of notable abandoned and forgotten structures in the Mojave's smaller towns that are well worth noticing.

Above: Dixie Inn. Hinkley, CA. 2015. Hinkley, California, is a town 14 miles northwest of Barstow, whose plight was detailed in the feature film *Erin Brockovich,* starring Julia Roberts. Released in the year 2000, the film described the efforts to expose the contamination of the town's groundwater by Pacific Gas and Electric Company (PG&E) with hexavalent chromium, a cancer-causing chemical. Despite massive remediation efforts since the 1990s, PG&E estimates that it will take approximately another thirty-five years before the cleanup is done. As a result, Hinkley, California resembles a ghost town today.

Harper Lake Road, Lockhart, CA. 2015

Storm Gate. Nipton, CA. 2016

Tank with New York
Mountains. Nipton,
CA. 2014

Spool, Kelso, CA. 2013

Green Room, Kelso, CA. 2014

Words of Wisdom. Cima, CA. 2014

GIANT ROCK

Down a long, bumpy, dirt road in the town of Landers stands what may be the largest freestanding boulder in the world. Giant Rock, as it is known, stands seven stories tall and occupies almost 6,000 square feet. It has an illustrious history which includes native rituals, purported German spies, and UFO conventions.

In the 1930s, a German immigrant prospector named Frank Critzer dug a hole under the Giant Rock and fashioned a 400-square-foot one-room subterranean apartment for himself, believing it would stay cool throughout the broiling Mojave summer. A short-wave radio enthusiast, he attached an antenna to the top of the boulder.

During World War II, Critzer fell under suspicion to be a German spy, and was killed under mysterious circumstances during a raid by local law enforcement. After his death, Critzer's dwelling was filled in with dirt and closed up. It is hard to consider a freestanding boulder to be an abandoned building, but that is exactly what Giant Rock is.

Giant Rock has long been thought of as the center of a spiritual energy vortex, dating back hundreds of years, when Hopi Native Americans held rituals there. In the late 1940s, Landers local George Van Tassel believed the vortex attracted extra-terrestrial aliens, with whom Van Tassel claimed to have contact with. By the 1950s, Van Tassel improved an old airfield next to the rock, built a café, and held UFO conventions, which attracted up to 11,000 visitors annually. Other than the Giant Rock, only the café's foundation remains.

Giant Rock. Landers, CA. 2016

Concrete Slab. Giant Rock, Landers, CA. 2014

Cabin. Lucerne Valley, CA. 2019

Cabin Interior. Lucerne Valley, CA. 2019

Red House. Lucerne Valley, CA. 2019

ZZYZX

Zzyzx Road can be reached from exit 239 off Interstate 15, about fifteen miles south of Baker, CA. It leads to a verdant oasis formerly known as Soda Springs. The name Zzyzx (pronounced zye-zicks) was fabricated by a radio-evangelist and self-proclaimed doctor named Curtis Howe Springer, who wanted the name of his new health resort to have the last word in the dictionary, and the last word in health.

A successful huckster, Springer used the radio to tout his homemade miracle cures for various ailments, from cancer to baldness. In actuality, his tonics were made of common vegetable juices and water.

Springer enrolled derelicts from Skid Row in Los Angeles to help build the Zzyzx Mineral Springs and Health Spa. They erected a sixty-room hotel, a chapel, an artificial pond with California Fan Palms and mineral bathhouses. Springer boasted on his national radio show about the unique restorative and healing effects of these hot springs and coaxed many to come to this obscure location from all over the USA. In reality, the water proved to be ordinary and heated by a hidden boiler. After an investigation in 1969, the American Medical Association called Springer "The King of Quacks," and exposed much of his false advertising. They could not remove his medical license, as it was found he never had one. Shortly thereafter, it was also discovered that Springer had no deed to the property, and was effectively squatting on the land. Springer and his followers were evicted in 1974, and the abandoned complex and land was reclaimed by the Bureau of Land Management. Many of the original buildings still stand, and have been repurposed as California State University's Desert Studies Center.

Guest Rooms. Zzyxx. 2017

Bath House. Zzyxx. 2017

Boat with Fan Palms. Zzyxx. 2017

Embedded Bratz. Lucerne Valley, CA. 2019

Green House. Randsburg, CA. 2014

8

LAKE DOLORES WATER PARK

What makes the desert beautiful is that somewhere it hides a well.

Antoine de Saint-Exupery

A water park in the hottest, driest desert in America? Sounds implausible, except for the proximity of underground springs which are fed by the massive Mojave Desert Aquifer.

In the early 1960s, a local entrepreneur named Bob Byers built a man-made lake, which he named after his wife, Dolores, off a desolate stretch of Interstate 15 in between Barstow and Las Vegas. Over the years, several elaborate waterslides, games, and attractions were added to the park, creating a bonafide tourist destination in the 1970s and 1980s.

The complex was sold in 1990, and rebranded as the Rock-A-Hoola Waterpark, which had a 1950s and 1960s rock-n-roll music theme. The new owners added jet-age graphics, and several new water-based attractions including a tube-rafting river ride. Television ads seen throughout Southern California called it the "Fun Spot in the Desert." In the end, long-term problems with profitability caused the park to close permanently in 2004.

Shortly thereafter, most of the water rides were dismantled and sold to other amusement parks and ventures. The main waterslide, the "Big Bopper" was taken apart and shipped to a water park in Canada. Over the years, the property has been consistently vandalized, with many of the buildings burned or gutted for their metal and copper wire. The husk of this large park, built for fun, lies hauntingly abandoned, covered in graffiti. It is slowly deteriorating, baking away in the hot Mojave sun.

Entrance. Lake Dolores Water Park. 2019

Turnstile. Lake Dolores Water Park. 2019

Plaza. Lake Dolores Water Park. 2019

Kiddie Slide. Lake Dolores Water Park. 2019

Kiddie Slide Detail. Lakc Dolores Water Park. 2019

Charred Building. Lake Dolores Water Park. 2019

Broken Sign. Lake Dolores Water Park. 2019

Window. Lake Dolores Water Park. 2019

9

DESERT CENTER

Any thoughts of guilt, any feelings of regret, had faded. The desert had baked them out.

Stephen King, *The Gunslinger*

Desert Center is a town off Interstate 10 in the southeasternmost portion of the Mojave's transition zone with the Colorado Desert. The town's existence was supported by several major projects, all of which have since come and gone. In the early 1930s, the Colorado River aqueduct was constructed, which brought more than 5,000 workers to the area. While in the region, geologists discovered a giant deposit of iron ore just 13 miles north of Desert Center. The industrialist Henry J. Kaiser set up one of the world's largest open-pit mining operations, known as the Eagle Mountain Mine. The mine operated at full production with over 4,000 workers through World War II, until Kaiser closed the mine down in 1982.

Desert Center also functioned as the southern gateway to General George S. Patton's Desert Training Center, where thousands of troops trained for battle in African desert conditions during the Second World War. The training center was removed by the end of 1944.

Today, Desert Center sits largely abandoned, with most of its 200 residents living in a retirement community on a man-made lake and golf course about two miles north of town. All of its businesses, including the elementary school and café, have been abandoned, except for the local branch of the United States Post Office.

Desert Schoolhouse. Desert Center. 2015

School Lunchroom. Desert Center. 2015

School Piano. Desert Center. 2015

Tractor. Desert Center. 2015

Star Sign. Desert Center. 2015

Red Van. Eagle Mountain. 2016

Family Café. Desert Center. 2012

Gas Pumps. Desert Center. 2012

10

THE HINTERLANDS

Across the desolation lay a supreme indifference, the casualness of night and another day, and yet the secret intimacy of those hills, their silent consoling wonder, made death a thing of no great importance. You could die, but the desert would hide the secret of your death, it would remain after you, to cover your memory with ageless wind and heat and cold.

John Fante, *Ask The Dust*, 1939

As you pass the eastern edge of Wonder Valley into the Sheephole Valley Wilderness on Route 62, signs of civilization become extremely rare. It can be quite disconcerting as the power poles and the lines that connect them vanish, and the promise of the sign leaving Twentynine Palms—"NO SERVICES 100 MILES"—become alarmingly apparent. There is, however, the unfettered glory of the open road, with untainted, capacious vistas and undulating hills to uplift the spirit.

Hinterland is a German word that means "the land behind," and in this case, the word is used to describe the easternmost fringes of the Mojave Desert. This is an area that can be so brutally hot, windy and deserted that a shrewd person realizes that a simple mistake can cost them their life. These are some of the most obscure and desolate places in all of California. By and large, it is an area that humanity has forsaken, and time has forgotten.

RICE, CALIFORNIA

Rice is a hard town to notice as you pass through it, because almost every trace of its existence has vanished. In its heyday in the 1930s and '40s, Rice reportedly had 5,000 residents, but now its population is zero. All that can be seen traveling east on Route 62 is a railroad spur with some neglected boxcars, some rubble of former buildings, the metal canopy of a former gas station and a very distinctive shoe fence. Rice has long been famous for being a distant location where travelers would leave pairs of shoes, first on a burned-out tamarisk tree, then on a nearby fence. Recently, people have begun tossing shoes on the metal canopy of the remnants of a former "76" gas station, which closed in 1982.

Much of Rice's most important history has been erased from sight. In the early 1940s, The U.S. Army established Desert Training Center, led by General George S. Patton, which trained soldiers for desert combat conditions just south of Route 62. A local airport was improved to create Rice Army Airfield, which featured two 5,000-foot runways, with barracks and support for thousands of men. This airport was used to train many of the pilots and crew for the invasion of Africa and Europe in World War II. By 1944, the airbase was decommissioned and repurposed for civilian use, until it was abandoned in 1958. Today, there is virtually no trace of this large endeavor visible from Route 62.

White Hot Stop. Rice, CA. 2013

Rail Shack. Rice, CA, 2015

Shoe Station. Rice, CA. 2019

Rice also is the home of the remains of the House of Koop, established July 10, 1794. While little is known about the House of Koop, the plaque that commemorates it indicates that it is what's left of what would be one of the oldest buildings in California.

YUCCA CRATER (LOWER RIGHT)

The Yucca Crater was an art installation created by Ball-Nogues studio in a desolate area beyond Wonder Valley. Standing 20-feet tall above the desert floor, the Yucca Crater was essentially a stylized swimming pool in which the viewer could take a dip as a reward for braving the long trip through the desert to experience it. The Yucca Crater was never completely finished and was left to deteriorate in the Mojave sun.

House of Koop. Rice, CA, 2015

Plaque Detail, House of Koop. Rice, CA. 2015

Yucca Crater. Old Dale, CA. 2012

Inverted Car. Iron Mountain Flats. 2015

Target Practice Car. Chubbuck, CA. 2015

1946 Ford Truck Grille. Cadiz Road. 2015

1946 Ford Truck Interior. Cadiz Road. 2015

TV Target. Iron Age Road. Old Dale, CA. 2016

BIBLIOGRAPHY

BOOKS

Abbey, E., *Desert Solitaire,* (New York, NY, Touchstone, 1968)

Fante, J., *Ask the Dust,* (Santa Rosa, CA, Black Sparrow Press, 1939)

Pepper, C., *Desert Lore of Southern California,* (San Diego, CA, Sunbelt Publications, Inc., 1999)

Stringfellow, K., *Jackrabbit Homestead: Tracing the Small Tract Act in the Southern California Landscape, 1938-2008* (Chicago, IL, The Center for American Places at Columbia College Chicago 2009)

WEBSITES

atlasobscura.com/places/zzyzx-mineral-springs-and-healing-center

brainyquote.com

cali49.com/mojave/2016/3/16/rice-cal

citylab.com/equity/2014/12/the-last-homesteads-of-wonder-valley-california/383372

deserttrainingcenter.com/history

desertusa.com/mojave-desert

digital-desert.com

ghosttowns.com/states/ca/rice

goodreads.com

lucernevalley.net/giantrock/

mojavedesert.net/desert-fever/san-bernardino-county

roadsideamerica.com/story/21414

wikipedia.org/wiki/Hinkley_groundwater_contamination

wikipedia.org/wiki/Lake_Dolores_Waterpark

wikipedia.org/wiki/Mojave_Desert

wikipedia.org/wiki/Owens_Valley

wikipedia.org/wiki/Palmdale,_California

wonderinthevalley.wordpress.com/about/small-tract-act-of-1938-2/

ABOUT THE AUTHOR

ANDY WILLINGER is an artist, photographer, writer and creative originally from New York City. As the son of a Madison Avenue creative director and the stepson of a photojournalist, he was raised to appreciate the importance of striking visuals and clever storytelling. Andy studied at Boston University, earning a B.S. degree in broadcasting and film. He came to California in 1990, where he fell in love with the capacious horizons of the desert and the sea, living in both Los Angeles and the Joshua Tree area. After establishing a successful career in television, Andy continues to be a devoted explorer of the delicate beauty and unforgiving desolation of the American Southwest. His photographs are collected and displayed worldwide.